Everyday Divine

Noel Sloboda

Červená Barva Press
Somerville, Massachusetts

Červená Barva Press
P.O. Box 440357
W. Somerville, MA 02144-3222

www.cervenabarvapress.com

Bookstore: www.thelostbookshelf.com

Cover Art: "Gossip" Eugene de Blaas (1843–1931)

Cover Design: William J. Kelle

ISBN: 978-1-950063-06-2

ACKNOWLEDGMENTS

Thank you to the editors of the following journals for publishing earlier versions of several of these poems: *Bete Noire* ("The Patron Saint of Rubberneckers": reprint), *Chaffin* ("The Patron Saint of Shoplifters"), *Confrontation* ("The Patron Saint of Universalists"), *Evansville Review* ("The Patron Saint of Abductees"), *Falling Star* ("The Patron Saint of Rubberneckers"), *Fjords* ("The Patron Saint of Truants"), *Fourteen Hills* ("The Patron Saint of Amateur Gardeners"), *Gargoyle* ("The Patron Saint of Piggy Banks"), *Grasslimb* ("The Patron Saint of the Forgetful"), *Harpur Palate* ("The Patron Saint of Commuters"), *I-70 Review* ("The Patron Saint of Preppers"), *Lindenwood Review* ("The Patron Saint of Cuckolds"), *Neon* ("The Patron Saint of Gossip"), *Off the Coast* ("The Patron Saint of Muscleheads"), *Sow's Ear Poetry Review* ("The Patron Saint of Audience Volunteers"), *Specs* ("The Patron Saint of Procrastinators"), and *Star*Line* ("The Patron Saint of Plagiarists"). *Waggle* ("The Patron Saint of Pharmaceutical Sales").

TABLE OF CONTENTS

"There are no saints, but there are also no sinners. There are people who are more saintly (vis-à-vis a particular strength of character) and those who are more sinful, but the differences are of degree and not of kind."

—Christopher Peterson, *Pursuing the Good Life*

Everyday Divine

The Patron Saint of Commuters

Forever coming or returning—
too intent on miles ahead to settle
for any single destination
let alone pause for conversation—
he keeps one bleary eye trained
on jagged lemon chiffon lines
just visible through the trees
dangling from his mirror—
sun-bleached pines that never grow;
the other eye glued to needles
telling him absolutely nothing
is wrong. He frets
about every little squeak and rattle
heard over the steady hum of rubber
on pavement. He fears the loss
of pressure in his Goodyears
and worries about the taint
of ethanol in his cylinders.
Usually concealed behind
a bug-speckled screen
halfway between today
and tomorrow, I once saw him
up close, propped against
a pump on sclerotic legs,
one dark hand on a nozzle,
the other pale and throbbing
as it choked the life out
of an invisible wheel.

The Patron Saint of Shoplifters

As if another strip search matters
if it keeps her fans happy—
never mind the critics, always

impossible to satisfy. She
giggles as she spins past a pair
of bored security guards

while gewgaws in her pockets jangle
and flashes of color escape
from under the hem of her billowing

sweatshirt. Burning behind
layer upon layer, she sacrifices
comfort for craft, starved for plaudits.

Fingers glimmering with fool's gold
flit across Italian silk scarves, plush
velour hats and calfskin bags. Long

forgotten is her first performance:
a 100 Grand bar filched
to fill a cramping belly—

before she hit marks between
row upon row of bright merchandise,
before she perfected this subtle art

of the lightning striptease in reverse,
before she knew somebody watched
behind every dressing room mirror,

before electronic eyes madly swiveled
whenever she exposed herself
to the spotlight's white-hot flame.

The Patron Saint of Plagiarists

Scuttles through dorm halls
during predawn hours

in search of that desperate glimmer
escaping from under a door—

the invitation for her
once more to brand

names of dead statesmen
on an inner forearm

or tattoo an algorithm
across a lifeline.

The Patron Saint of Muscleheads

Barricaded in our cellar
my brother quickly lost count of reps
as he wheezed and writhed

like an electrified eel
atop a gunmetal bench, pumping
fists toward heaven, while rusty

York plates clanged
like chains on a Victorian
ghost. He groaned red prayers

seeking blessings for dumbbells
that squeezed the baby fat
and smiles from his face,

gnarled his fingers into brambles
so he couldn't dial a phone,
expanded the nave of his ribcage

into a massive temple of self-
loathing, the swarm of doubts inside
buzzing so loudly they drowned out

dulcet tones of our stepmom
when she tried to call him
back to the world above.

The Patron Saint of Truants

Once stooped to press
an ear to the ground
grinning as the late train rolled
toward an unlucky president.

Later puffed and hacked
under bleachers, flushed
cheeks half-hidden
behind a smokescreen of Kool.

These days mostly stays
tucked away at home,
lips pursed, cheeks sallow,
after bowing for hours

to cornflower blue deities
trapped in a puny box.

The Patron Saint of Amateur Gardeners

Every April the stories changed,
though our rituals remained the same
as I sealed beds behind Oma's place,
blanketing rain-soaked ground
under layers of black and white—
a foundation for mulch to follow.

Oma saved papers for months,
stacked headlines about ice storms,
holiday sales and pep rallies
atop plow ads and obits.
As I laid out pages capturing
everything that mattered most
during the shortest days of the year,
I made sure all perfectly aligned
to ring the house with a winter hex
warding off spring weeds.

This rough magic never took hold,
never prevented eruptions of thistle
and oxalis I spent May weekends
ripping out. Oma supervised my labors
and muttered German curses—
more *macht nichts* words
scratched into memory if powerless
over profaned ground.

The Patron Saint of Pharmaceutical Sales

Off balance in velvet

mauve Miu Miu stilettos
that make her feel

close to heaven, she totters

across hospital tile, gelid
smile firmly in place

dispensing samples

wrapped in superlatives:
the latest chewable breakthrough,

artificially-sweetened game-changers,

a classic cure now in gel form—
miracles all, not to be swallowed

on an empty stomach.

The Patron Saint of Preppers

Somebody who sounds just
like my childhood best friend
calls about another hand cannon
he has bought for the day
when gas is gone.

He insists his ammo will last
three years, maybe four,
and he has extra weapons
to share with unfortunates like me
who don't heed the signs:

Korean solar cars, dropping
gold prices, rising red
meat costs, stagnant birth-rates
among Pandas. When he rings
long after midnight, I imagine myself

protesting: I am busy picking
remains of yesterday's devotions
from between my teeth.
I might confess I have no idea
how to release a safety—

let alone fix other survivors
in crosshairs. But I never
stop him; I always listen
while he exalts Lugers and Rugers;
Goblins, Berettas, and Kalashnikovs.

Livid names from his armory
clatter across the distance between us
accompanied by the clang of brass
he juggles as he loads once more
for the end of the world.

The Patron Saint of the Forgetful

Abandons his station
beside mother's bedside

and stalks empty halls
during weekly visits—

black wingtips clacking
on bleached linoleum

tapping out secret messages
I have given up

trying to decipher
before I disappear again.

The Patron Saint of Audience Volunteers

Before velvet ascends, I tilt
forward in my seat, left arm
aquiver. I was born
to rap knuckles against
the bottom of an upturned hat
and listen for an echo. I cannot
separate bronze rings, nor can I undo
aluminum manacles. My gaze
faithfully tracks the pendulous
swing of a golden pocket watch.
My right hand clutches a hair
plucked from my scalp, perfect
for testing a blade's edge.
Command me to cluck like a chicken
when I shimmy across the stage
like the ghost of Elvis.
Cram me into a wooden box
and slice me in half. After
I am pieced back together
I will keep your ciphers
forever sealed in my vaults.

The Patron Saint of Cuckolds

After another half night
entwined, I catch my last
glimpse of you before you

transform afresh:
soft curves of hips
rewritten by pinstripes,

delicate feet crushed
into patent leather pumps
black as asphalt. You

practice this art of seduction
in reverse before every vanishing
while I remain still as a hare

fixed in headlights, trapped
under the freight of the comforter
and hours ahead—

the impossible interval
between now and when
you might return to slip

off this daytime disguise
I try so hard to believe
I alone can see through.

The Patron Saint of Piggy Banks

Cast from the first clay
she smolders like the harvest moon

while countless stout disciples
stashed in corners of toy chests

or buried beneath socks
faithfully wait for the summons

of her wrathful squeal—
the rallying cry for all to mutiny

and topple bleached spires
harboring feckless brutes

who swing hammers
on rainy days.

The Patron Saint of Alien Abductees

Splayed across the sidewalk as if
dropped from heaven, he rattles
change in a plastic cup, swears
he still sees flashes of green
from a Venusian tractor beam
every time he closes his eyes.
The kink in his neck from scanning
the night sky has become impossible
to unknot. He has not slept for weeks
but promises once he does—
and recovers from loss of blood
drained in a lab inside the Moon—
he will share incontrovertible proof
of his journeys through space:
an extraterrestrial canticle
laced with gamma rays and stardust
foretelling the future of the cosmos—
as astonishing as it is expansive
even if it only half makes sense
since he learned it light-years from here
and it was composed for a mouth
with three tongues.

The Patron Saint of Universalists

Lavishes French kisses

on starving lingerie models
and bloated lepers alike.

Always says never imagine

this will not happen
again. Does not know

what to do about the dead

pixels on the flat screen
like noctilucent clouds

hanging on the horizon.

The Patron Saint of Gossip

Back when she followed me
around during fourth grade—

that last year mom cut my hair—
I believed she loved me.

Nowadays, I rarely see her:
she burns daylight

hours online, posting
on countless message boards,

always hidden behind an alias—
her true name as impossible

to discover as her home base.
Yet even swaddled in secrecy,

she still receives invitations
to all the best parties in town.

Fashionably late, she hovers
on thresholds, letting hot air

escape into the night
while her voice insinuates itself

between guests and hosts,
shrill and tremulous as a cat

imitating birdsong.

The Patron Saint of Rubberneckers

You vow to yourself: never
again will you succumb
to the tyrannical spell
of mere curiosity.

And so you forget
about him, secreted
behind the driver's seat
for weeks on end, silent

and still while you roll
back and forth from work
crisscrossing byways—
until shards of glass

spill across blacktop
and catch flashes of blue;
or an upside-down tanker leaks
gallons of goo that smells

like moldering meat;
or a splash of crimson
stains the grill of a car
the same make and model as yours.

Tender but unspeaking,
he splays a warm palm
across the top of your skull
and as your spine jellies

your head swivels, turning
and turning until it feels
as though your neck must
snap. Then you speed up—

free once more to pretend
you are alone, refocus
on markers ahead and
fume about lost time.

The Patron Saint of Procrastinators

Like a late March thaw

he nibbles another crust
of yesterday slathered in jam

made from good

intentions. He will return
after a siesta

enveloped in enormous wings

yellowed and stiff
from disuse. Trussed

in dreams he is

worshipped by a clowder
of housecats bathing

in afternoon sun.

ABOUT THE AUTHOR

Noel Sloboda earned his Ph.D. from Washington University in St. Louis. His dissertation about Edith Wharton and Gertrude Stein became a book. He sat on the board of directors for the Gamut Theatre Group for a decade, while serving as dramaturg for its nationally recognized Shakespeare company. Sloboda has published two poetry collections, six chapbooks, and hundreds of poems in journals and magazines. He is currently an Associate Professor of English at Penn State York.

www.ingramcontent.com/pod-product-compliance
Lightning Source LLC
LaVergne TN
LVHW041929090826
845145LV00017B/2781

* 9 7 8 1 9 5 0 0 6 3 0 6 2 *